AF226004

BABES AND BLOSSOMS

BABES AND BLOSSOMS

Original
Verses by
Walter Copeland
Drawings by
Charles Robinson

Edited & revised by
Duncan Brown

SiliconBloom

First published in the UK in 2024 by SiliconBloom
an imprint of Electronic Dream Plant Limited.

Electronic Dream Plant Limited connect the digital to the analogue
with works of fiction, wisdom and knowledge published worldwide
from EDP Global HQ nestled in Chipping Norton
in the heart of the Oxfordshire Cotswolds.

The Electronic Dream Plant can be found online @ edp.earth

Cataloguing in Publication Data
is available from the British Library

ISBN 978-1-0687749-0-4

Graphic design, layout and typography by Ole Makkesen Designlab

For Enneke

ANEMONE

The Anemone grows in woods and meadows. The
first flowers show their white and pink faces in March
when the strong winds blow, but they always turn
their backs to the wind. The name Anemone means
Wind-flower.

BRAMBLE

The Bramble grows in the hedgerows and in waste
places. It climbs over fences, and hooks itself on other
plants by its strong curved prickles. Its flowers may be
seen through the summer, but most people prefer to
look for its fruit, the blackberry.

BUTTERCUP

Buttercups grow beside the daisies in almost every
field. The flowers, which are as yellow as butter, may
be seen all the summer. They have a bitter taste, so
cattle will not eat them.

CANTERBURY-BELLS

The Canterbury-Bell has flowers like little bells. It
likes the sunshine, and its flowers bloom all the
summer. The bees are fond of them, and go right
inside the bells.

CHERRY

Cherry-blossom makes the trees white in April and May. Some kinds of Cherry-trees grow wild in the woods, and the birds eat the fruit when it comes, as they eat it in our gardens and orchards too if we do not drive them away.

CHRYSANTHEMUM

Chrysanthemums make our gardens gay in the autumn, when most other flowers have died or gone to sleep for the winter. Some kinds cannot bear the cold, and must be planted in pots and taken indoors before Jack Frost is about.

CLOVER

The Clover grows all the summer in fields and at the road-side. It helps to make hay sweet, and cattle like to eat it. Its green leaves grow in groups of three, unless you are very lucky and you find one with four leaves.

COWSLIP

The Cowslip likes to grow in damp meadows. It carries a bunch of yellow flowers on a tall stalk, and its leaves are crinkled. It comes in April and May.

CROCUS

The Crocus pushes its head above ground in early spring. It opens its cup-shaped flower when the sun shines and does not mind the cold winds, but if a cloud passes over the sun it closes its flower quickly to keep it dry in case the rain or snow may come.

DAFFODIL

In some places the Daffodil grows wild in meadows
and pastures, but most of us see the pretty flower
only in our gardens, nodding its yellow head in the
spring winds.

DAISY

Everyone knows the Daisy, it grows almost
everywhere, and like the gorse is always in bloom.
It opens its flowers in the light, and closes them
when it begins to grow dark, so it is called Daisy
which means Day's Eye.

DANDELION

The Dandelion grows wild everywhere, and would
make itself at home in the garden if we did not root
it out. Its yellow flowers come in March and stay
until October.
When the flowers wither, we see the fluffy round
balls of seed called Dandelion Clocks.

FLAG or Iris

The wild Flag or Iris grows in ditches, or beside
streams, with its roots in the water.
Other kinds grow in the garden. All have long narrow
leaves with sharp edges which look like green swords.
They are summer flowers.

FORGET-ME-NOT

The Forget-Me-Not grows beside streams, and in
other wet places, from spring to autumn. Its flowers
are blue, as everyone knows, but the buds are pink.
Its green leaves shine as if they were wet.

GERANIUM

The Geranium will grow in the garden in summer,
but it cannot bear the cold. So if we want to save our
plants we must put them in pots and bring them
indoors when the warm days are over.

GORSE

Gorse, or Whin, or Furze, is never out of bloom.
A few of its golden flowers may be found on any day
in the year, but the best blooming-time is in April
and May. Instead of leaves it has sharp prickly spikes.

HAREBELL

The dainty little Harebell grows on heaths and
pastures, and may be seen swaying to and fro in the
breeze from July to September. In Scotland it is
called the Bluebell.

HEATHER

Heather grows on moors, commons, and hillsides.
It covers the ground like a bright carpet in autumn,
and is very springy to walk upon. Its flowers are tiny,
but there are so many of them that they often make
a whole hillside quite purple.

HONEYSUCKLE

The Honeysuckle grows in the hedges and woods.
We may find its trumpet-shaped flowers in the
summer and autumn. We like it for its sweet scent,
and the bees like it for its honey.

JESSAMINE

The Jessamine is a garden shrub. It will climb upon a
wall or fence. One kind has white flowers which come
in summer, and another has yellow flowers which
bloom in winter. The flowers look rather like stars,
and smell very sweet.

LILY

There are many kinds of Lilies. Some of them are
in bloom all the summer.
Most kinds grow in shady parts of the garden, and
are very tall and beautiful. They are not all white.
Some wear bright colours, and one has markings
something like those on a tiger.

LILY-OF-THE-VALLEY

The white bells of the Lily-of-the-Valley can
sometimes be found in woods, but the flower grows
more often in shady places in gardens. Bees notice
its strong sweet scent and visit it often, but they do
not find any honey in it.

LONDON PRIDE

London Pride or None-so-Pretty is easy to grow. It
has many tiny pink flowers, and will make our gardens
look gay in May and June, even in smoky towns.

LUPIN

The Lupin shows its bright flowers in May and June.
They have a sweet scent. Its beautiful green leaves are
like hands with many fingers, which it closes and
hangs at its sides when it goes to sleep at night.

MARGUERITE

Some people call the Ox-eye Daisy, the Marguerite.
It makes the hayfields and railway banks white in
May and June, and keeps in flower until August if
it is not cut down by the reapers.

MARIGOLD

The Marigold's deep yellow flowers may be seen in
the garden in the late summer. It does not mind the
hot dry weather which makes some other plants
wither, and will sometimes go on blooming until Jack
Frost comes.

MAY

In May and June, the May-tree or Hawthorn bears so
many white flowers that it looks almost as if it were
covered with snow. The flowers have a strong scent.

NASTURTIUM

The Nasturtium is a useful plant in the garden, for it
climbs well and will cover an ugly fence or a heap of
rubbish all the summer, if we plant it near them in
the spring. Its strange round leaves are rather like
shields, and its flowers like helmets.

PANSY

The Pansy's flowers are something like little faces,
and seem to be looking at us. They are of many
beautiful colours, and look as soft and smooth as
velvet. They show their faces in the garden all
through the summer.

PEONY

The splendid Peony, with its large crimson, or pink,
or white flowers, likes to grow in the sunshine.
It makes our gardens gay in May and June, and is
tall and strong.

PINK

The Pink is not always pink, but has many colours.
It has a very sweet scent. The first flowers show
themselves in our gardens in June, and they last
a long time.

POPPY

The bright red flowers of the Poppy can be seen in
the corn-fields, and on railway banks, and waste
places, from June until September.
There is no honey in the fine flowers, but their hairy
stalks are full of a bitter juice.

PRIMROSE

We know that spring is here when we see the
Primrose.
Its pretty yellow flowers and crinkled green leaves
come in crowds to the woods in April and May.

ROSE

June is the best month for Roses, but they can be
found in our gardens all the summer, and even at
Christmas a few show their faces. There are many
kinds of garden roses, but they have all come by
change after change from the little wild rose which
scrambles over the hedges.

SNOWDROP

The Snowdrop is one of the first flowers to wake
from its winter sleep.
It comes in January, sometimes pushing its head
through the snow. It grows in meadows and orchards
as well as in the garden.

SUNFLOWER

The Sunflower may be seen in the garden all through
the summer. It lifts its round golden face, which is
something like the sun, high above most of the other
flowers. The smallest kinds of Sunflower are as tall as
a little child, and the largest are taller than a man.

SWEET-PEA

The Sweet-Pea is a climbing plant with a sweet scent.
Its beautiful flowers of many colours look something
like butterflies. It blooms in our gardens at the end of
June, and will go on doing so all through the summer
if we are careful to cut off all the faded flowers.

SWEET BRIAR

The Sweet Briar is a kind of rose. It grows wild, but is
often planted in hedges and gardens, because of the
sweet smell of its small leaves and flowers. Its little
pink roses bloom in the summer.

THISTLE

The Thistle is to be found in almost every hedgerow
and field in the late summer and autumn. It is not
easy to pick its purple flower, which is guarded by
prickly green leaves.

THRIFT

Sometimes we see the Thrift or Sea-Pink in garden borders, but its real home is on the rocks and cliffs of the sea-shore, and on the rocky sides of high mountains. It makes these grey places gay with its pink flowers and leaves like grass. We may see it at any time from April until October.

TULIP

The Tulip is a kind of lily. The first Tulips come in the garden when the crocuses are going, and other kinds follow, so we may see their flower-cups of many colours for quite a long time.

VIOLET

The sweet Violet is liked by everyone because it smells so nice. Its purple flowers come in March and April, and again in the autumn. It grows wild in woods and on banks in some places, but is more often seen in the garden.

WALLFLOWER

The Wallflower or Gillyflower is a favourite because of its strong sweet scent. Some kinds of Wallflower will grow in cracks upon a wall, but those that grow in the garden beds are stronger and larger. It blooms from April right into summer.

WATER-LILY

The Water-Lily grows in pools and slow-moving rivers. Its root is in the mud at the bottom of the water, but the broad green leaves float upon the water, and the beautiful white or yellow flowers are lifted above it. It blooms from June to August.

BABE WINNIE says,
"I will call here and see
If they have

an

W HEN Baby Nellie went
for a ramble,
She scratched her finger
picking the

Bramble

TO see if you really
love butter hold up
Just under your chin
a gold

BABY CISSIE delightedly
tells
How the fairies from the
dells
Ring the

BABE CHARLIE says
it makes him merry
To see the blossoms
of the

B ABE BELLA said,
"Oh, Bertie, come
And buy
a red

BABE PAT and Babe Ann
will go over and over

A field

in search of a

four-leaved

BABY BEE said,
"Off we'll now slip
Into the fields
to gather

BABY MAY cried,
as she woke us,
"I have found
an early

PRETTY little Baby Bill
Picked this
yellow

BABY TOMMY has
his eye on
The very largest

BABE PETER was so very lazy He would not stoop to pick a

BABY BOB, the comical wag,
Says he's devoted
to the

LIKE the eyes of our dear
little Baby Tot
Are the flowers
of the
dainty

THE Baby cries,
"Oh give me some
Of that
          bright red

Geranium

BABE TIMMY says
he'll take his horse
And bring home
lots of
yellow

"COME here and see",
said Baby Nell,
"The daintily hanging,
sweet

THE littlest babe would
smile and chuckle
If you should
not know

Honeysuckle

BABY BOBBY wonders

whether

If he walks out

he'll find

some

BABE IDA says,
"Just see how fine

Is our sweet

climbing

BABY TOMMY delightedly cried

When he saw

the

London Pride

BABE JENNIE and her brother Billy Are going hunting for a

THIS merry little
Sister Sally
Has plucked

a

Lily-of-the-Valley

BABE FRED cried
when he found his hoop in
The midst of
a bed of
flowering

Lupin

B ABE MARGARET says that
she thinks the most sweet
Of all her
sweet flowers
is the

BABE DORIS says
if she must carry gold
It will be in the
shape of a
bunch of

Marigold

THE Babes all think it
sweet to play
Under the blossoms
of the

May-tree or Hawthorn

BABE POLLY cried,
"Oh, sister, come
And we
will
pick

BABE PATSY, let your
sister Ann see
The delicate bloom
of your

beautiful

BABE BELLE is glad
when she can see any
Peeping buds
on the great big

Peony

BABE CLARA says,
"I really think
No flower
is sweeter than
the

BABY SAMMY
got quite soppy
Seeking in
wet fields
a

SOME Babes like better
by far than the trim rose
The pale yellow blooms
of the

woodland

BABE ROSABELLE says
that she knows
The sweetest flower
is the

BABE JOAN to her sister
says, "Oh, oh, drop
That silly grass
and take
a

B ABE NORAH says,
"I'll be in an hour
And bring with me
a big

BABE BERTHA says,
"I'll go and see
If I can find
a fresh

ALL Babes like to go
in the lanes to admire
The beautiful blooms
of the wild

BABY DICKIE gave a whistle
When he plucked
a prickly

Thistle

BABE JIMMY says
he'd like to lift
Into his plot
a root
of

BABY BETTY said
she knew lips
Weren't so red
        as scarlet

Tulip

L ET me come, Babe Di,
oh! let
Me come, and pluck
a

${B}$ABE MYRA says, "Look at
this pretty dear tall flower;
It must be, I think,
just a
    sweet-smelling

THE very venturesome
Baby Billy
He waded
        for a

Time for bed
Sleepy head

www.ingramcontent.com/pod-product-compliance
Lightning Source LLC
Chambersburg PA
CBHW041729030726
47636CB00012B/511